おやつとごはん 100枚 レターブック

100 writing and crafting papers :
Foods and Sweets

はじめに

『100枚レターブック』は、1枚ずつ切り離して使える紙を100枚綴じた本です。
この本では、16名のクリエイターによる「おやつとごはん」をテーマにした50柄を集めて、1柄につき2枚ずつ収録しました。
つるつる／ざらざら、真っ白な紙／クリーム色の紙／黄色いクラフト紙など、質感や色の異なる6種類の紙に刷られた、多彩な「味わい」をお届けします。

「ひと味違う」便せんとしてはもちろん、お気に入りの1枚を壁に貼って気軽なインテリアとして楽しんだり、ぽち袋作りやちょっとしたラッピングなどにもお使いいただけます。
お祝いのメッセージにケーキのページ。宴席のお礼の一言にはやっぱりビールと枝豆の柄にしようか。そういえば、あの人の好物はなんだろう……。

その日の気分や、贈る相手に合わせてお好きな紙を選び、ご自由にお楽しみください。

パイ インターナショナル 編集部

使用上の注意

・ページをしっかり開き、紙をゆっくり引っ張るときれいにはがれます。
・筆記用具によっては、インクがにじむことがあります。

Foreword

100 Writing and Crafting Papers contains 100 sheets of paper that can be cut out and used individually.
Sixteen creators were commissioned to provide a total of 50 designs on the theme of snacks and meals, with two sheets allocated to each design.
The result is a veritable smorgasbord of patterns, printed on six types of paper of different colors and textures, including silky smooth and rough, white/cream-colored/ yellow-craft paper.

The sheets here can be used as writing paper with a twist, of course, but a favorite design can just as easily be stuck on a wall to add a personal touch to a room, or used to make little bags, or as wrapping paper for a special small something.
Pick a cake page for a congratulatory message, or perhaps a beer and edamame design for a party thank-you note. Or maybe that person's favorite food...

Choose paper that suits your mood that day, or the recipient. Most of all, have fun!

The editers PIE International

Notes

・Open pages out wide and pull gently to remove neatly.
・Ink from some writing implements may run or spread.

手紙に……
For letters

ラッピングに……
For Wrappings

インテリアに……
For Interiors

クリエイタープロフィール
The artists

柿崎サラ カキザキサラ

桑沢デザイン研究所卒業。広告制作会社のデザイナーを経て、イラストレーターとして活動中。2014年、LUMINE meets ART AWARD エレベーター部門 ルミネ賞・オーディエンス賞を受賞。
sarakakizaki.jimdo.com

Sara Kakizaki
Graduate of the Kuwasawa Design School. Following a stint as an advertising agency designer, became an illustrator. 2014 winner of LUMINE Audience Award, Elevator section, at the LUMINE meets ART AWARD.
sarakakizaki.jimdo.com

kanaexpress カナエクスプレス

高校卒業後渡英。ロンドンの大学で版画技術やグラフィックデザインを学ぶ。現在はケシゴム版画での作品制作やイラスト提供を行っている。
kanaexpress.blogspot.com

kanaexpress
Traveled to the UK after high school and studied printmaking and graphic design at university in London. Currently produces eraser prints, and illustrations.
kanaexpress.blogspot.com

かよくらふと 田中嘉代 タナカカヨ

イラストレーター、デザイナー。2010年より京都でアトリエ兼ショップ「かよくらふと」を営む。季節や日常の愛しいものをイラストにし、使って楽しくもらって嬉しい、ちょっときもちがゆるむような雑貨づくりを心がけている。
instagram.com/kayochop

Kayo's craft shop / Kayo Tanaka
Illustrator and designer. Since 2010 has run "Kayo's craft shop" studio and store in Kyoto. Turns the seasonal and adorable into illustrations, striving to create subtly soothing everyday items that are fun to use and delightful to receive.
instagram.com/kayochop

小井田由貴 コイダユキ

版画家。東京都生まれ、武蔵野美術大学短期大学部卒業。木版画を用いた新しい表現で、装画・テキスタイル・パッケージデザインなど様々な分野で活動中。北欧をはじめとする世界各地の暮らしを想起させる作品で、人気を博している。
yukikoida.com

Yuki Koida
Printmaker. Born in Tokyo, graduate of Musashino Art University Junior College of Art and Design. Works in various fields including cover design, textile and package design, creating new looks with woodblock printing. Her works evoking everyday life in Scandinavia and elsewhere have proven extremely popular.
yukikoida.com

小関祥子　コセキショウコ

切り絵やコラージュの技法で作品を制作するイラストレーター。カレンダーの制作をきっかけに紙雑貨を作りはじめ、現在では雑誌や企業キャンペーンなど幅広いジャンルで活躍している。かわいいけれど甘すぎない、すっきりした大人っぽい印象の作品が人気。

kittari-hattari.strikingly.com

Shoko Koseki

Illustrator who uses cutout and collage techniques in her work. Making a calendar launched a career in paper goods, and she now works across various domains from magazines to corporate campaigns. Her work is popular for its crisp, grownup aesthetic: cute without being sickly sweet.

kittari-hattari.strikingly.com

嶽 まいこ　ダケマイコ

イラストレーター／漫画家。1985年石川県生まれ。2008年金沢美術工芸大学視覚デザイン専攻卒業。"日常の中のふしぎなモノ・コト"をテーマに、ものづくりを行う。出版物に『なんてことないふつうの夜に』（祥伝社）などがある。

dakemaiko.com

Maiko Dake

Illustrator and manga artist. Born 1985 in Ishikawa. Majored in visual communication design at Kanazawa College of Art, graduating in 2008. Makes things on the theme of "the unusual in everyday life." Books include *On Ordinary Nights* (Shodensha).

dakemaiko.com

砂糖ゆき　サトウユキ

イラストレーター／グラフィックデザイナー。神奈川県在住。関東を中心に活動中。日常の出来事や食べ物をあたたかいタッチで描く。おいしいイラストレーションを得意としている。

momoimo514.tumblr.com

Yuki Sato

Illustrator/graphic designer. Lives in Kanagawa, works mainly in the Kanto area. Depicts everyday happenings, food etc. in imagery with a cozy feel. Specializes in illustrations of the tasty sort.

momoimo514.tumblr.com

とみこはん

消しゴムはんこを彫って押して絵を描く、消しゴム版画・イラストレーター。食べ物や人物のモチーフを中心に、温かみのある作風で、雑誌、書籍、テレビ、広告など様々な分野で活躍。全国各地で消しゴムはんこの楽しさを伝えるワークショップ講師としても活動中。

www.tomikohan.com

Tomikohan

Illustrator, maker of eraser prints using erasers carved into stamps to form pictures. Has a distinctive heart-warming style featuring mainly food and people as motifs; works in numerous fields including magazines, books, television and advertising. Also runs workshops across Japan showing people how to have fun with eraser stamps.

www.tomikohan.com

tomozoo トモゾー

イラストレーター。「ユーモアで楽しく、見た人が笑顔になるようなイラスト」をモットーに2014年より活動開始。店舗印刷物のイラストデザイン等を中心に、オリジナルのポストカードや個性的な雑貨の制作も行っている。
tomozoo.jimdo.com

tomozoo

Illustrator since 2014 committed to supplying illustrations that are "funny and fun, and bring a smile to the faces of those who see them." Produces original postcards and distinctive merchandise with a focus on illustrated designs for in-store/restaurant printed material.
tomozoo.jimdo.com

ナカミサコ

北海道出身、東京都在住。女子美術大学プロダクトデザイン専攻卒業。グラフィックデザイン会社のデザイナーとして勤務後、フリーランスで活動中。服や靴、食べ物を描くことを得意とする。
miminaka.tumblr.com

Misako Naka

Originally from Hokkaido, resides in Tokyo. Majored in product design at the Joshibi University of Art and Design. Worked as a designer for a graphic design firm before going freelance. Specializes in drawing clothing, shoes and food.
miminaka.tumblr.com

ヌトグラン

イラストレーター。「なんだこれ！ でもかわいい」をテーマに、どうぶつっぽくておもちゃっぽいイラストやマンガ、グッズを制作している。挿画や雑貨デザインなどの仕事で活動中。
nutoguran.com

nutoguran

Illustrator. Produces animal-like, toy-like illustrations, manga and merchandise with a "Don't know what it is, but it's cute!" vibe. Works in illustration, and design for household items/sundries.
nutoguran.com

はらぺこめがね

原田しんやと関かおりによる夫婦イラストユニット。食べることが大好きで「食べ物と人」をテーマに活動中。挿絵や絵本制作、ワークショップの講師など、絵を描くことをなりわいとしている。
harapekomegane.com

Harapekomegane

Illustrator couple Harada Shinya and Seki Kaori are enthusiastic foodies producing work on the theme of people and food. Whether it's illustrations and picture books, or running workshops, drawing pictures is what they do.
harapekomegane.com

bubuchiyo　ブブチヨ

造形家。埼玉県出身。Twitterに絵日記を投稿する事を日課にしている。毎年1月に、東京で張り子の展示販売を行う。

twitter.com/bubuchiyo

bubuchiyo

Papier-mache artist, from Saitama. Posts a daily illustrated diary on Twitter. Every January displays and sells papier-mâché figures in Tokyo.

twitter.com/bubuchiyo

松園量介　マツゾノリョウスケ

1984年生まれ。イラストレーター。カラーインクを使い制作。都内を中心とした展示、雑誌の挿し絵、アパレルブランドへのイラスト提供などを中心に活動。

matsuzonoryosuke.com

Ryosuke Matsuzono

Illustrator, born 1984. Uses colored inks. Exhibits his work, mainly in Tokyo; is employed primarily in magazine illustration, providing images for clothing brands etc.

matsuzonoryosuke.com

安福 望　ヤスフクノゾミ

1981年生まれ、兵庫県神戸市出身のイラストレーター。好きな短歌や川柳にちなんだ絵を発表する活動を続けている。著書に『食器と食パンとペン わたしの好きな短歌』（キノブックス）などがある。

syokupantopen.jugem.jp

Nozomi Yasufuku

Illustrator from Kobe, born 1981. Produces pictures named after his beloved tanka and senryu poetry. Books include *Tableware, Breads & Pens "My Favorite Tanka"* (Kinobooks).

syokupantopen.jugem.jp

山中玲奈　ヤマナカレナ

イラストレーター、東京都出身。CM制作、出版／デザイン、印刷会社勤務を経て、2015年よりフリーランスとして独立。広告、書籍、雑誌を中心に幅広く活動の他、CINRA.STOREにてグッズを展開。独自の視点から描かれる軽妙なタッチと鮮やかな色彩が特徴。

www.renax.tokyo

Rena Yamanaka

Illustrator from Tokyo. Following a career in commercials, publishing/design and a printing firm, turned freelance in 2015. Does work for advertising, books, magazines and more, and has merchandise on CINRA.STORE. Drawn from a unique perspective, her works are distinguished by their witty touch and vibrant colors.

www.renax.tokyo

おやつとごはん 100枚レターブック

2018年11月15日　初版第1刷発行
2025年 2月14日　　第3刷発行

編著　パイ インターナショナル
翻訳　パメラミキ
編集・ブックデザイン　佐野彩子

発行人　三芳寛要

発行元　株式会社 パイ インターナショナル
〒170-0005　東京都豊島区南大塚2-32-4
TEL 03-3944-3981　FAX 03-5395-4830
sales@pie.co.jp

印刷・製本　TOPPANクロレ株式会社

ISBN 978-4-7562-5141-1 C0070
Printed in Japan

100 writing and crafting papers : Foods and Sweets

Designed by 16 Japanese Artists

Witten and edited by PIE International
English translation : Pamela Miki
Photography : Daisuke Matsumura
Editing & book design : Ayako Sano

Published by : Hiromoto Miyoshi

PIE International Inc.
2-32-4 Minami-Otsuka, Toshima-ku,
Tokyo 170-0005 JAPAN
sales@pie.co.jp

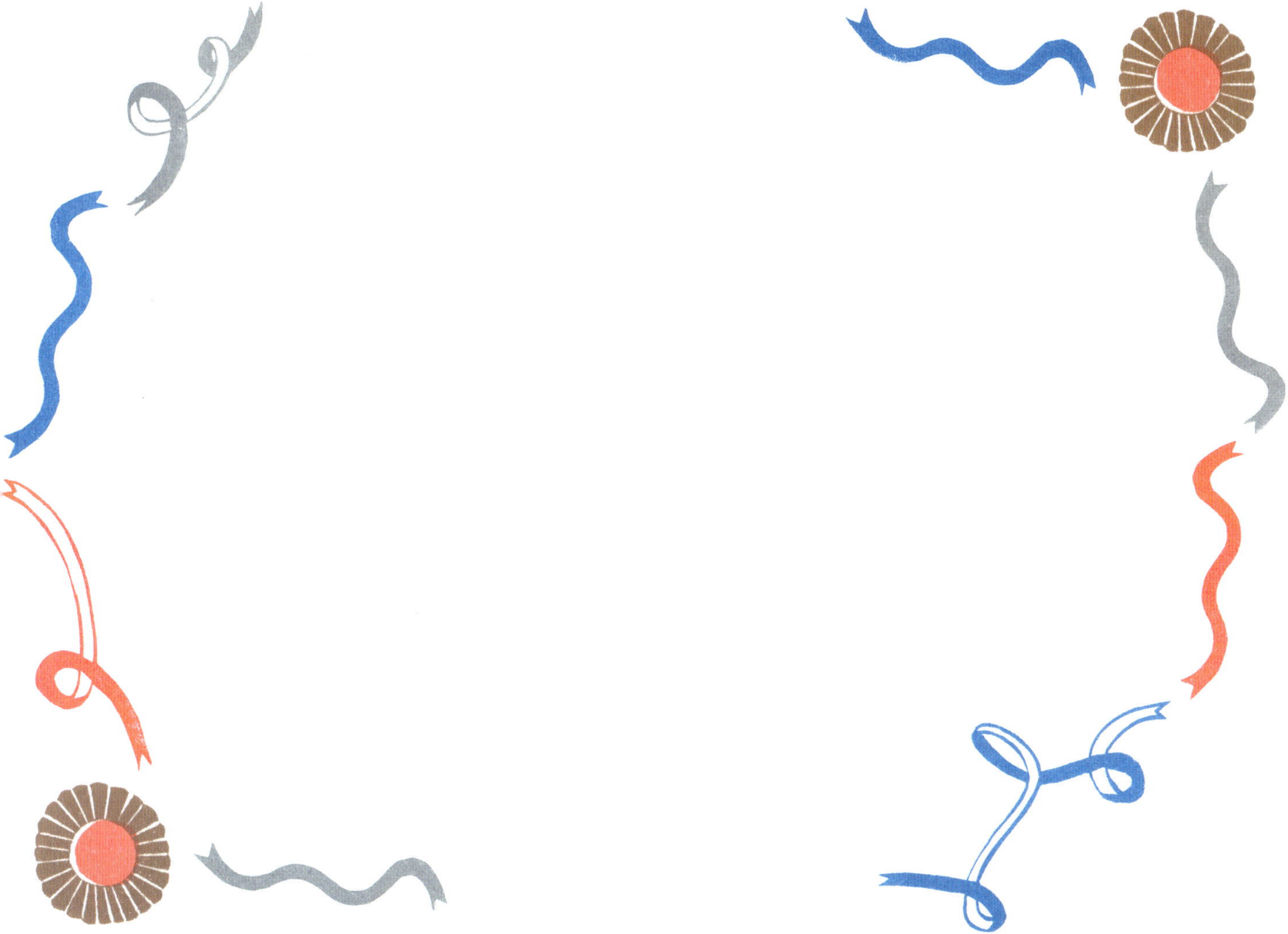

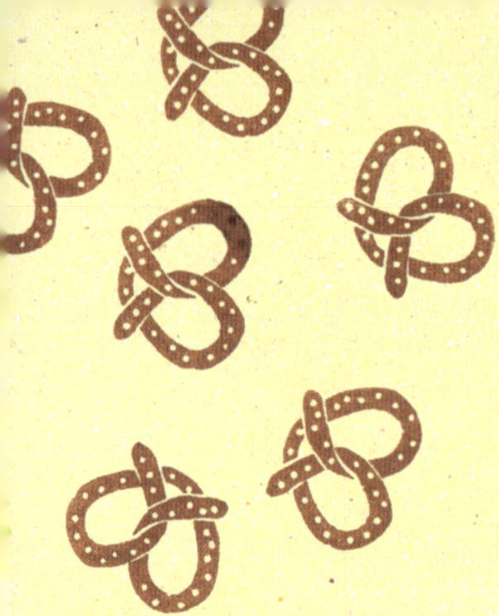

Wonder Restaurant

Special Raw Fish Caught by Little Chef

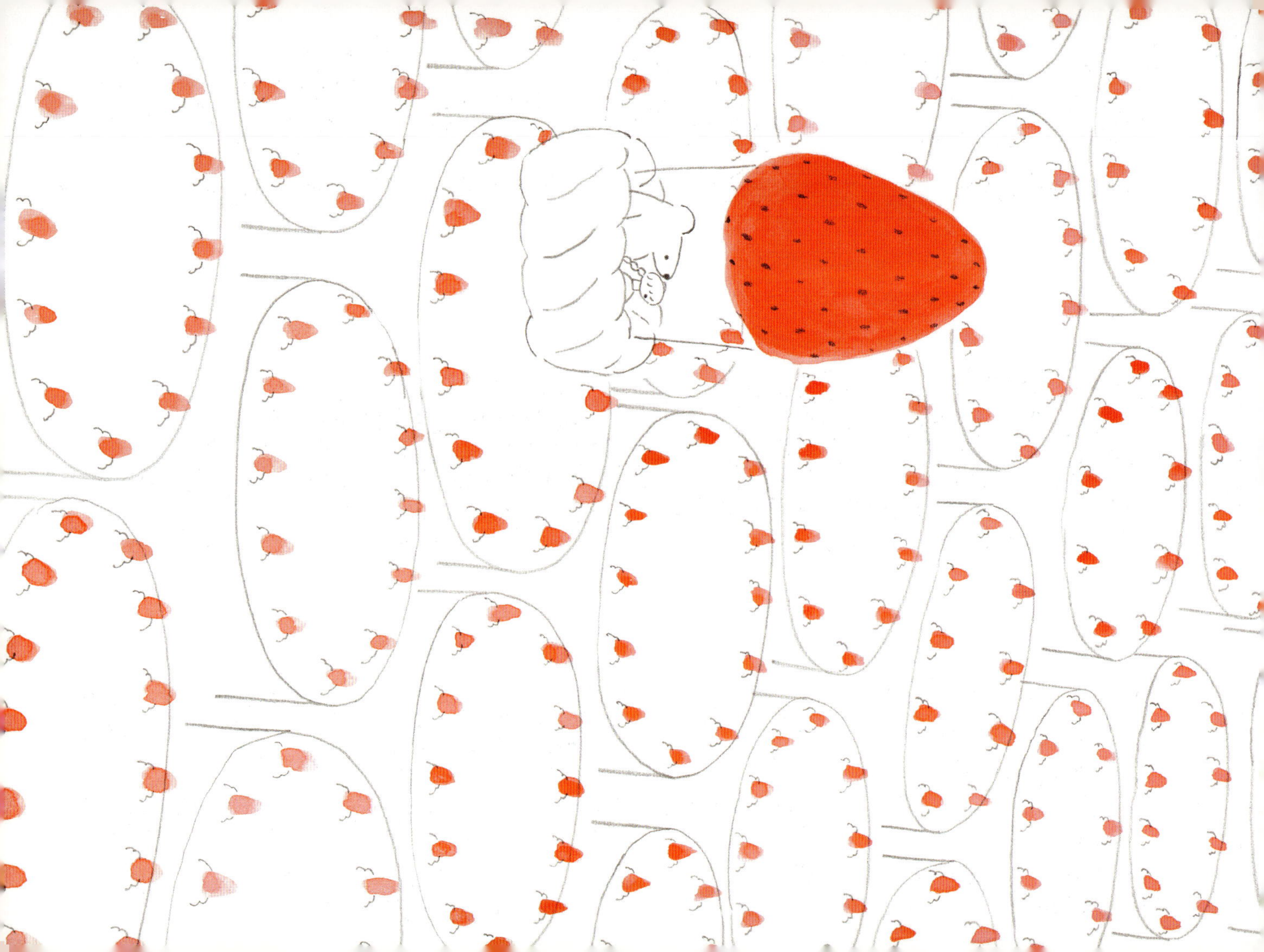

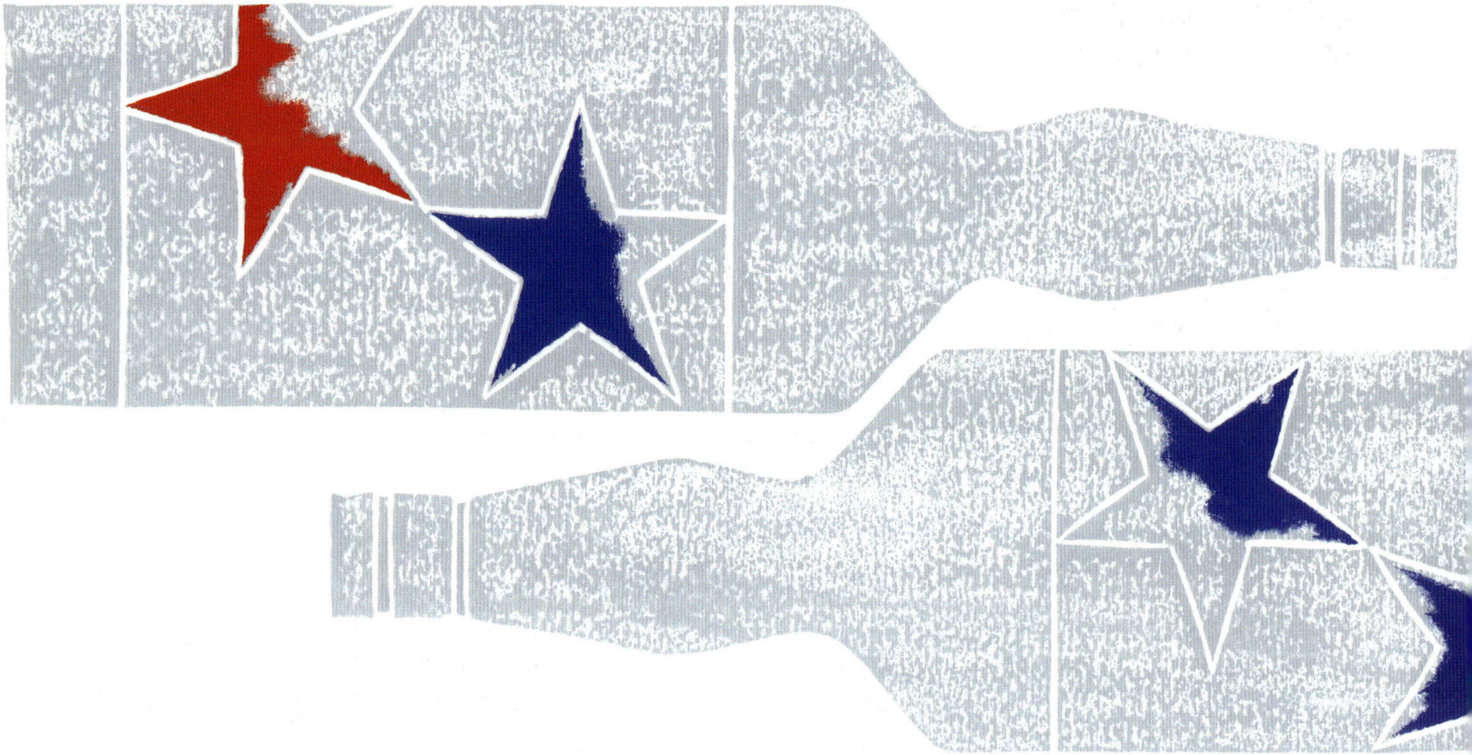

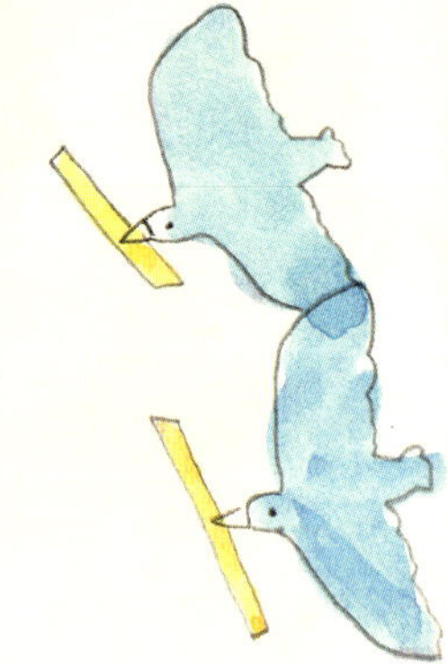

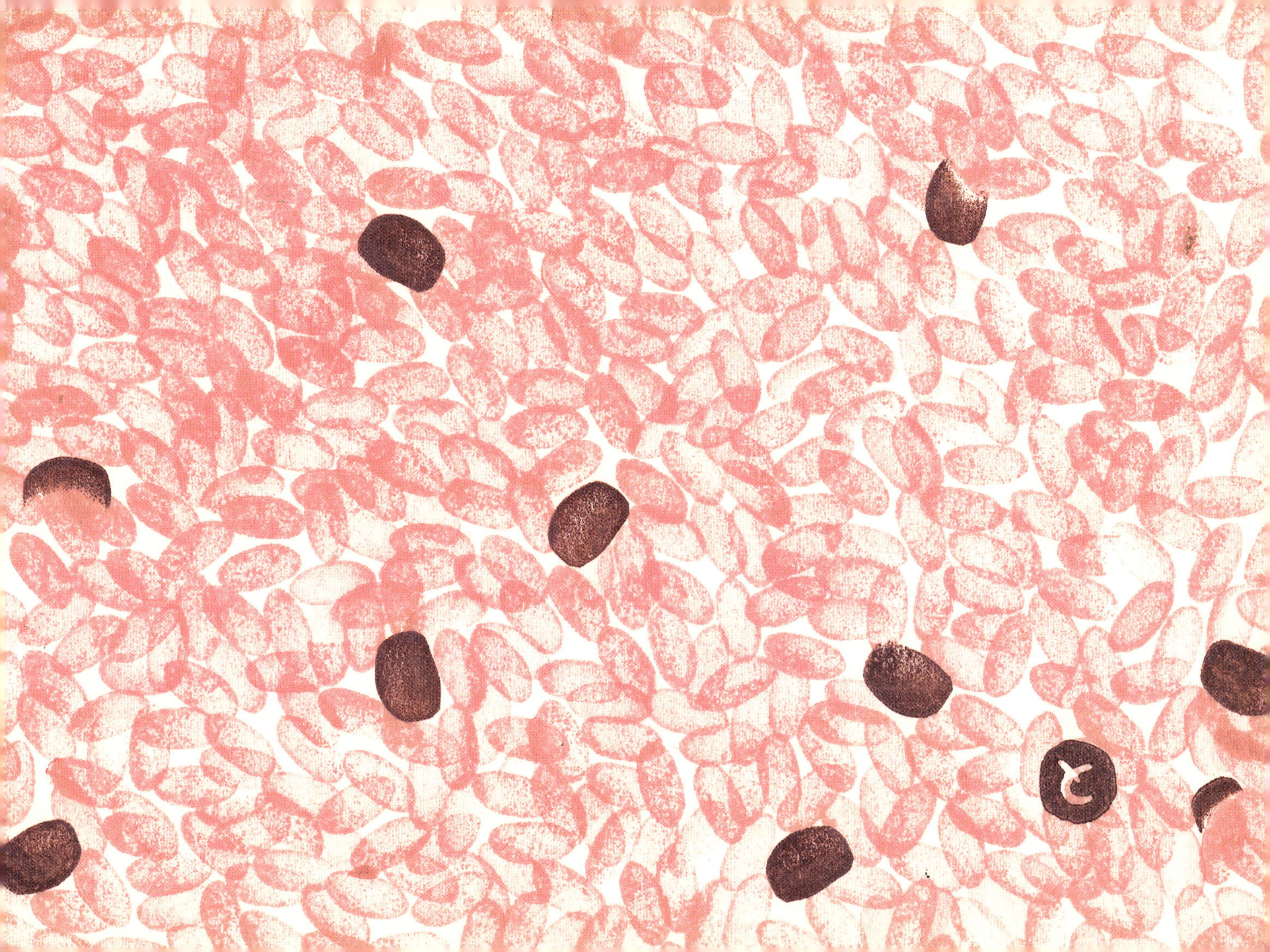

Wonder Restaurant

Chocolate Fountain

Wonder Restaurant

Tea time Cup Coffee

POTATO

CURRY

CURRY

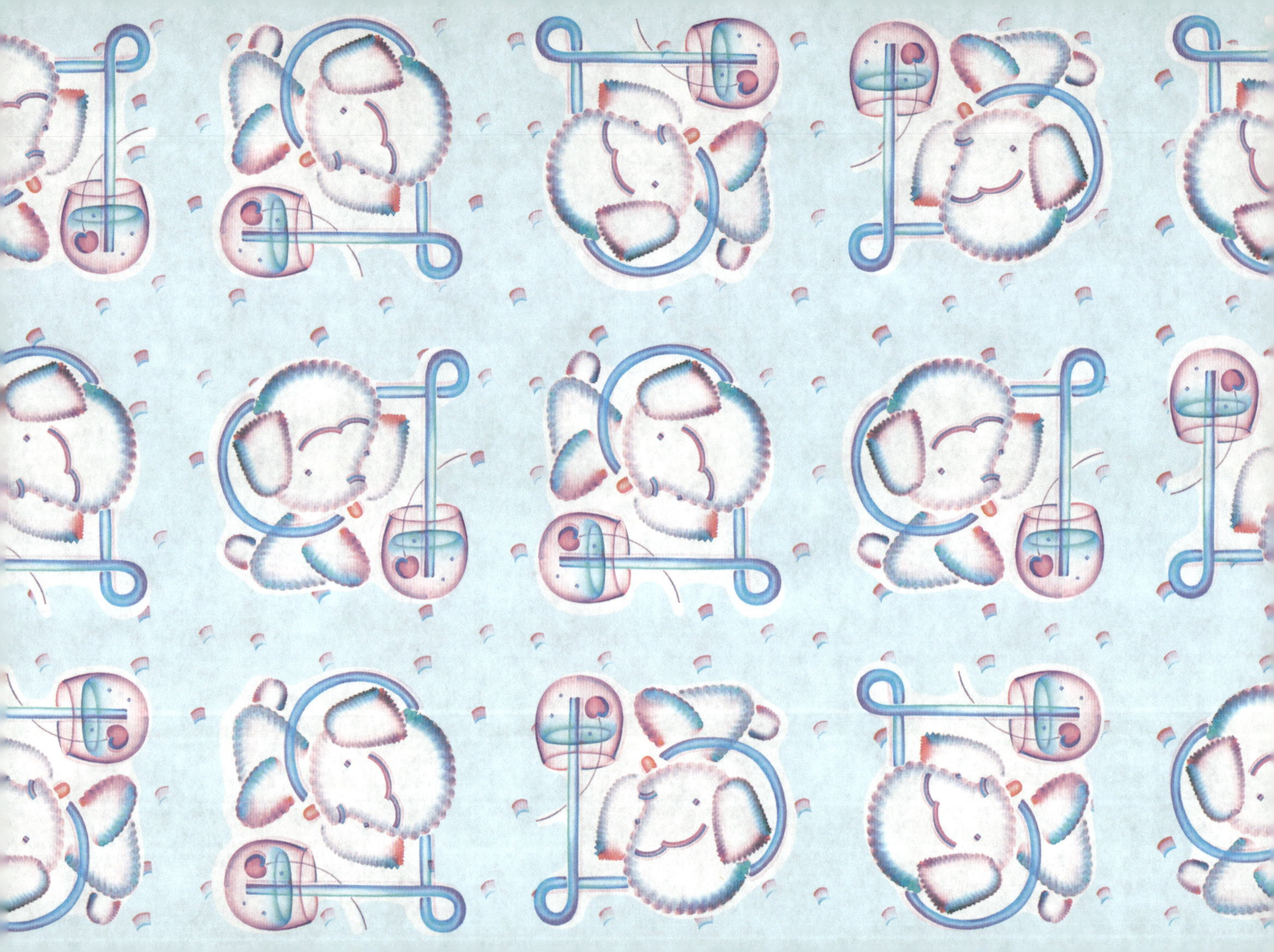

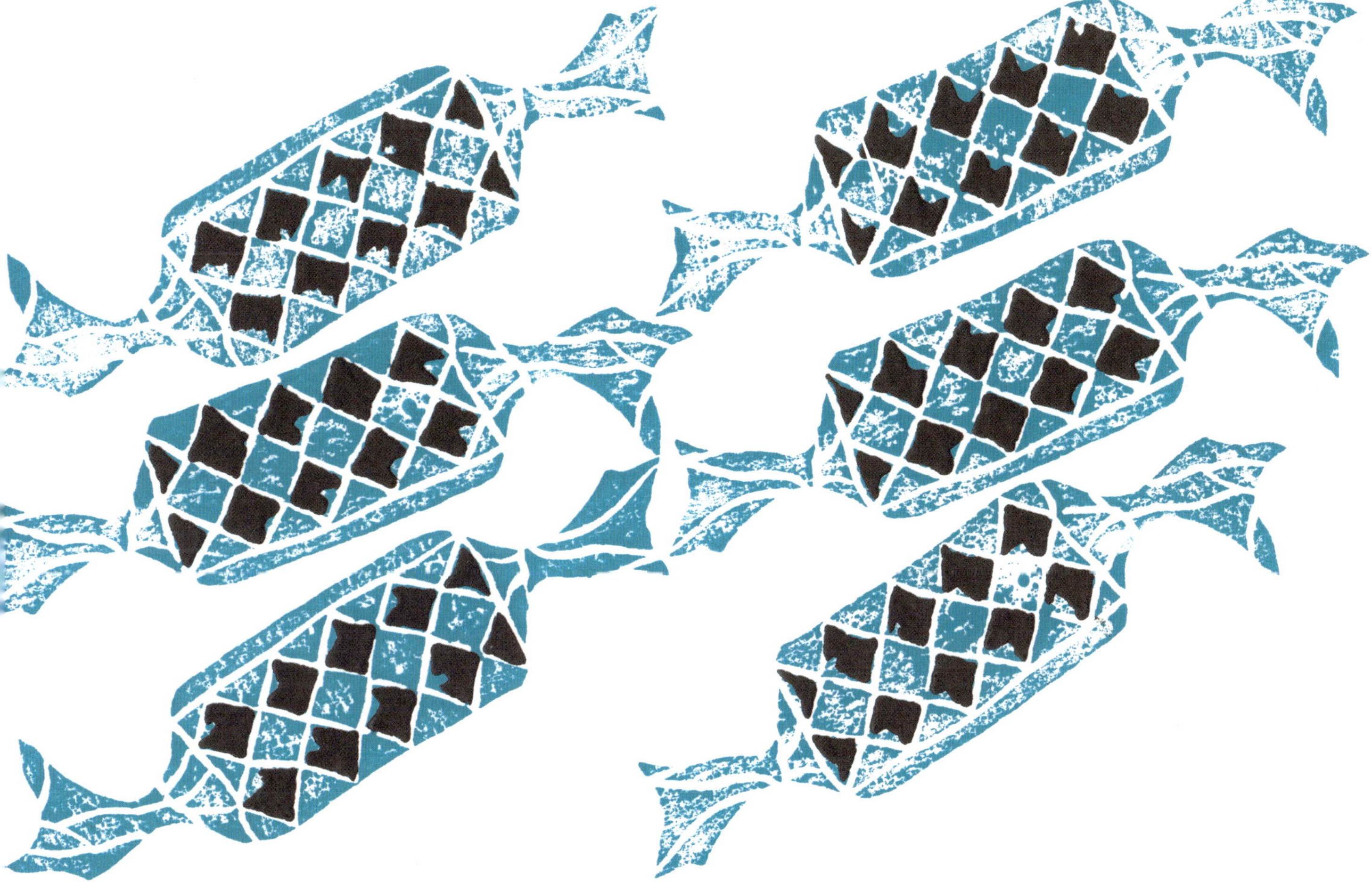

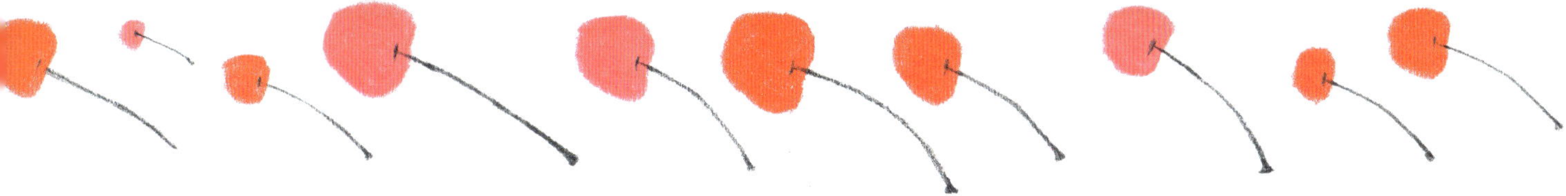

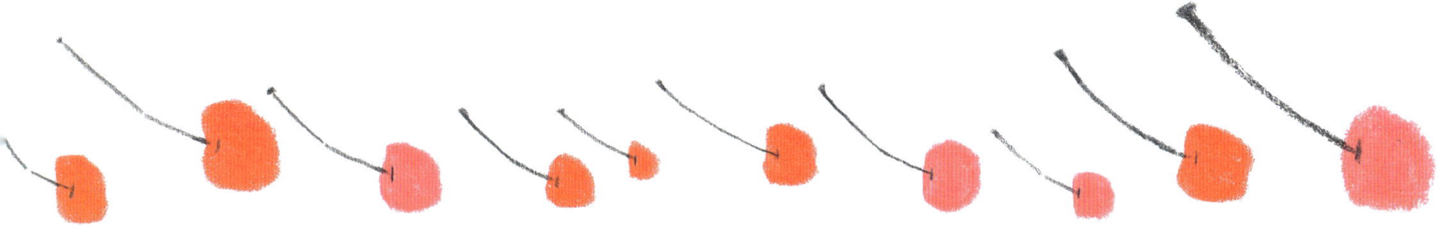

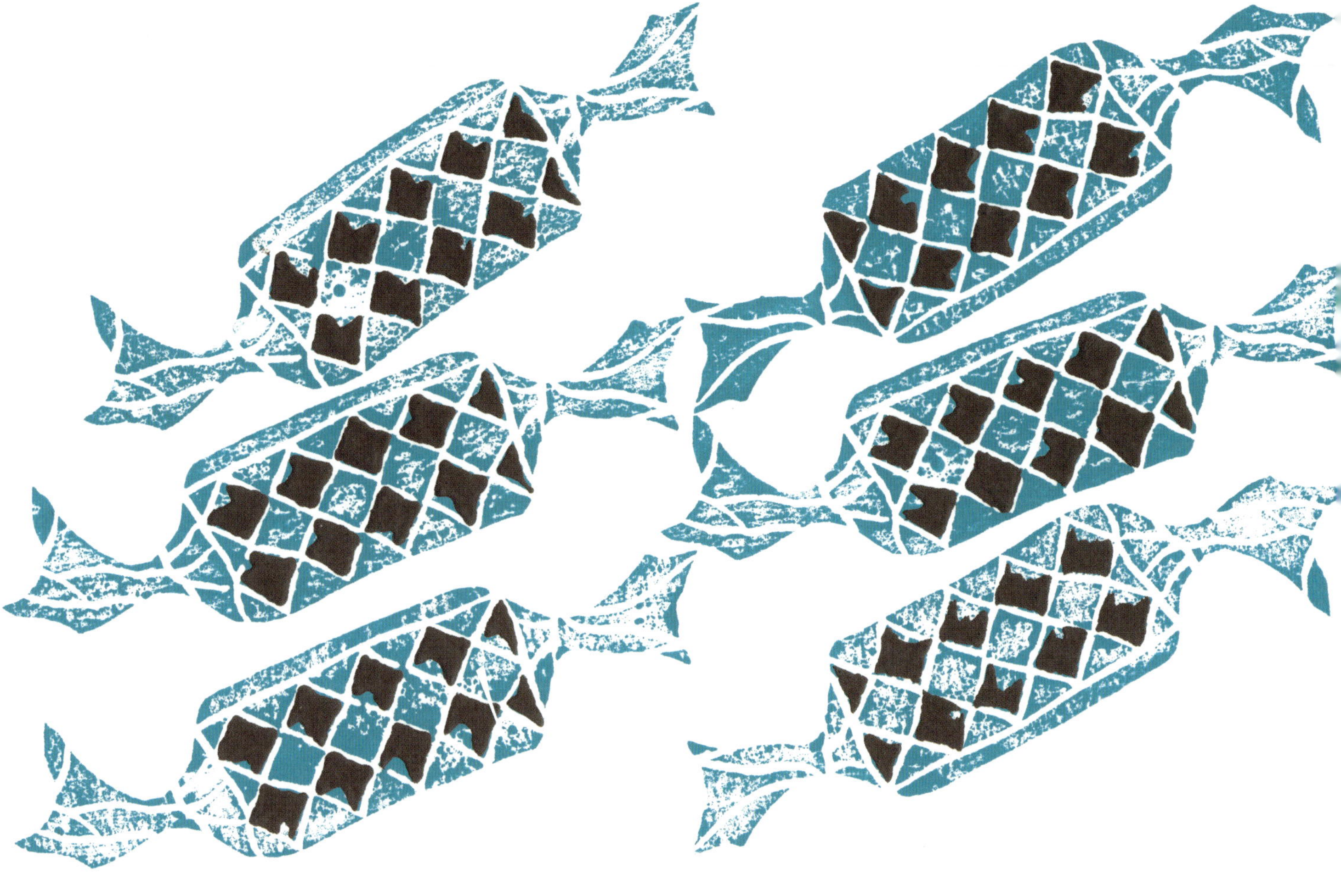

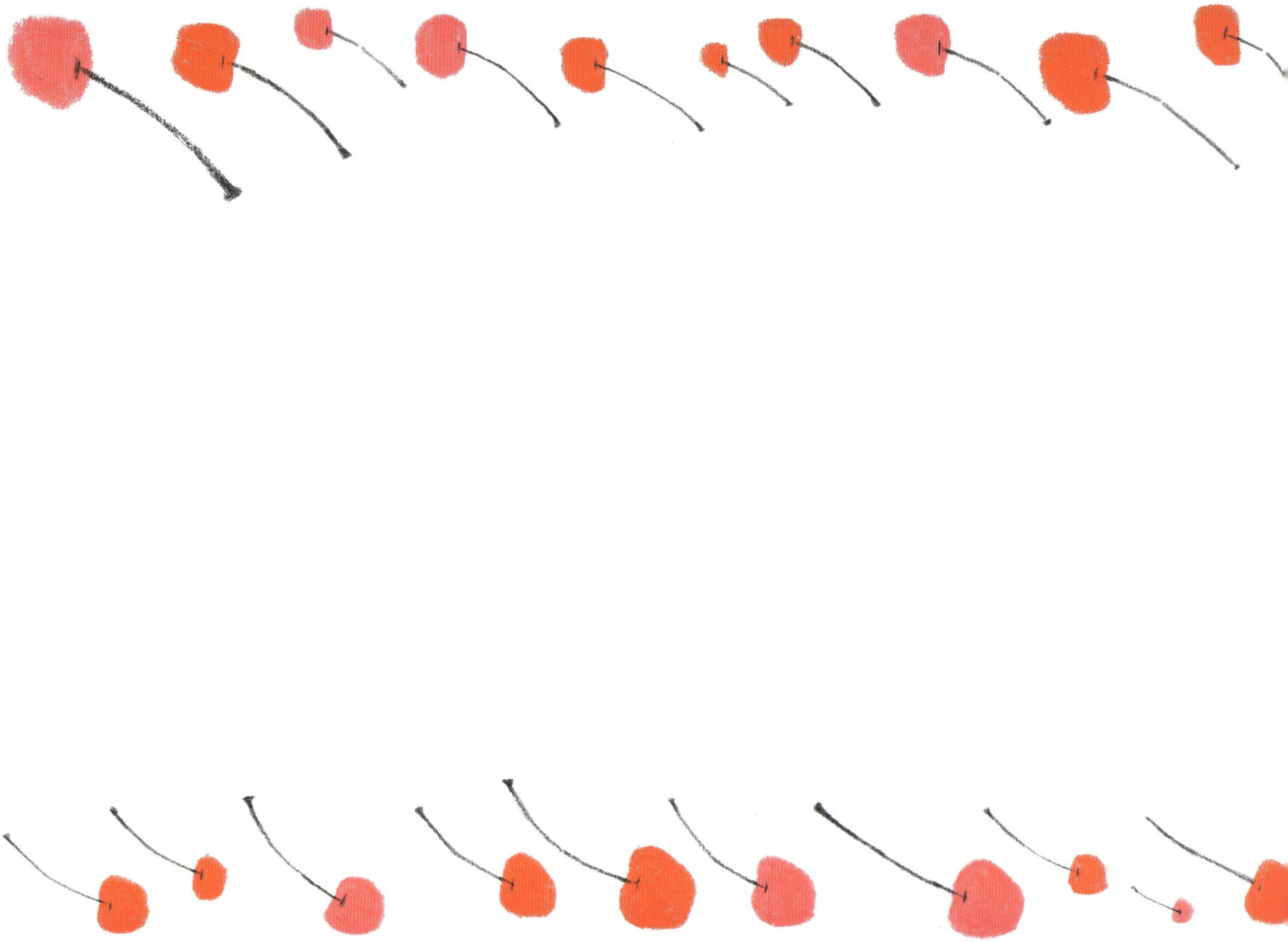

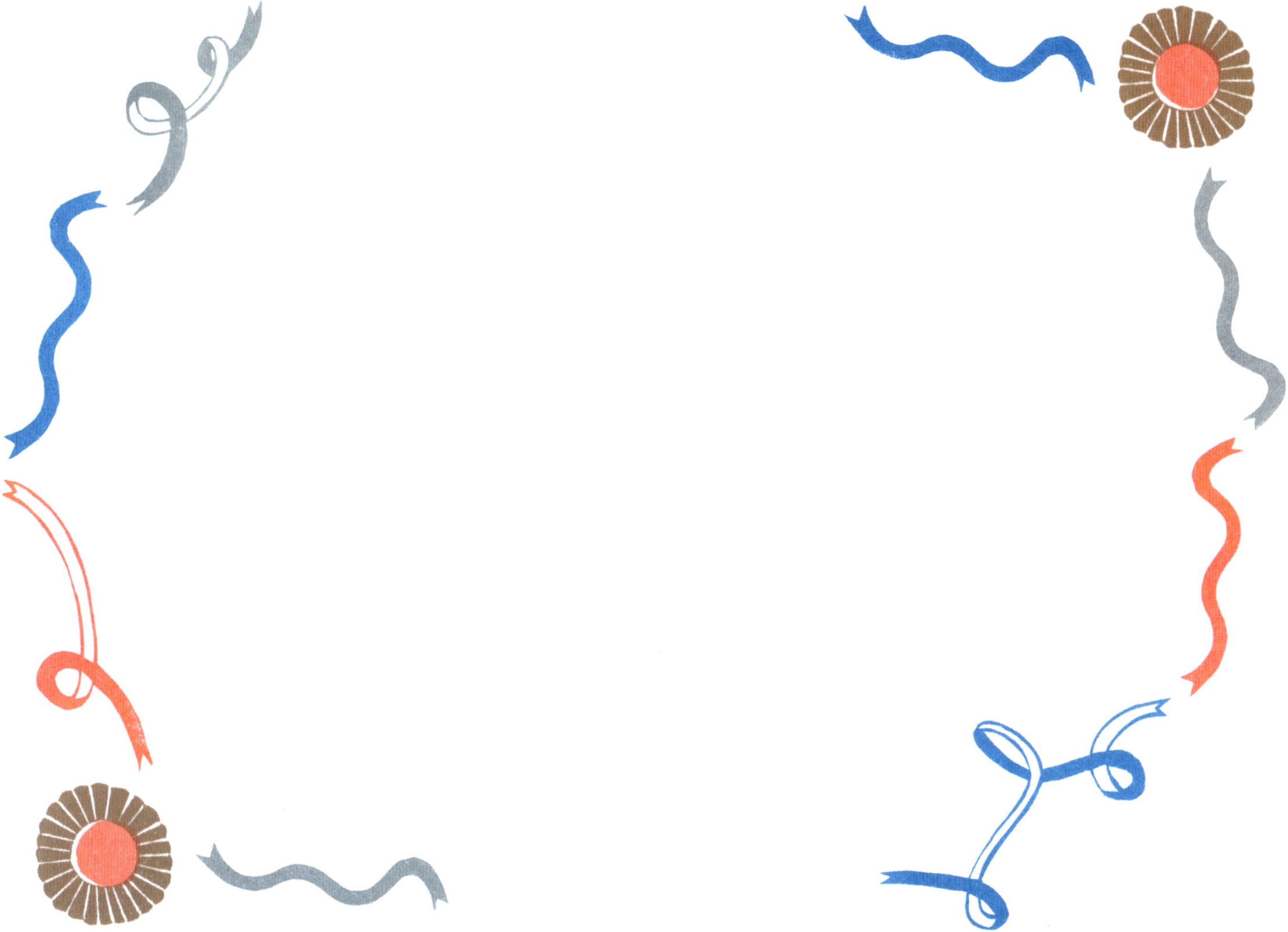

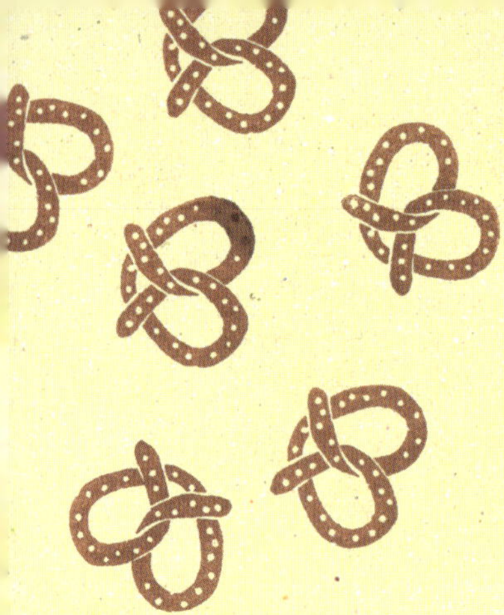

Wonder Restaurant

Special Raw Fish Caught by Little Chef

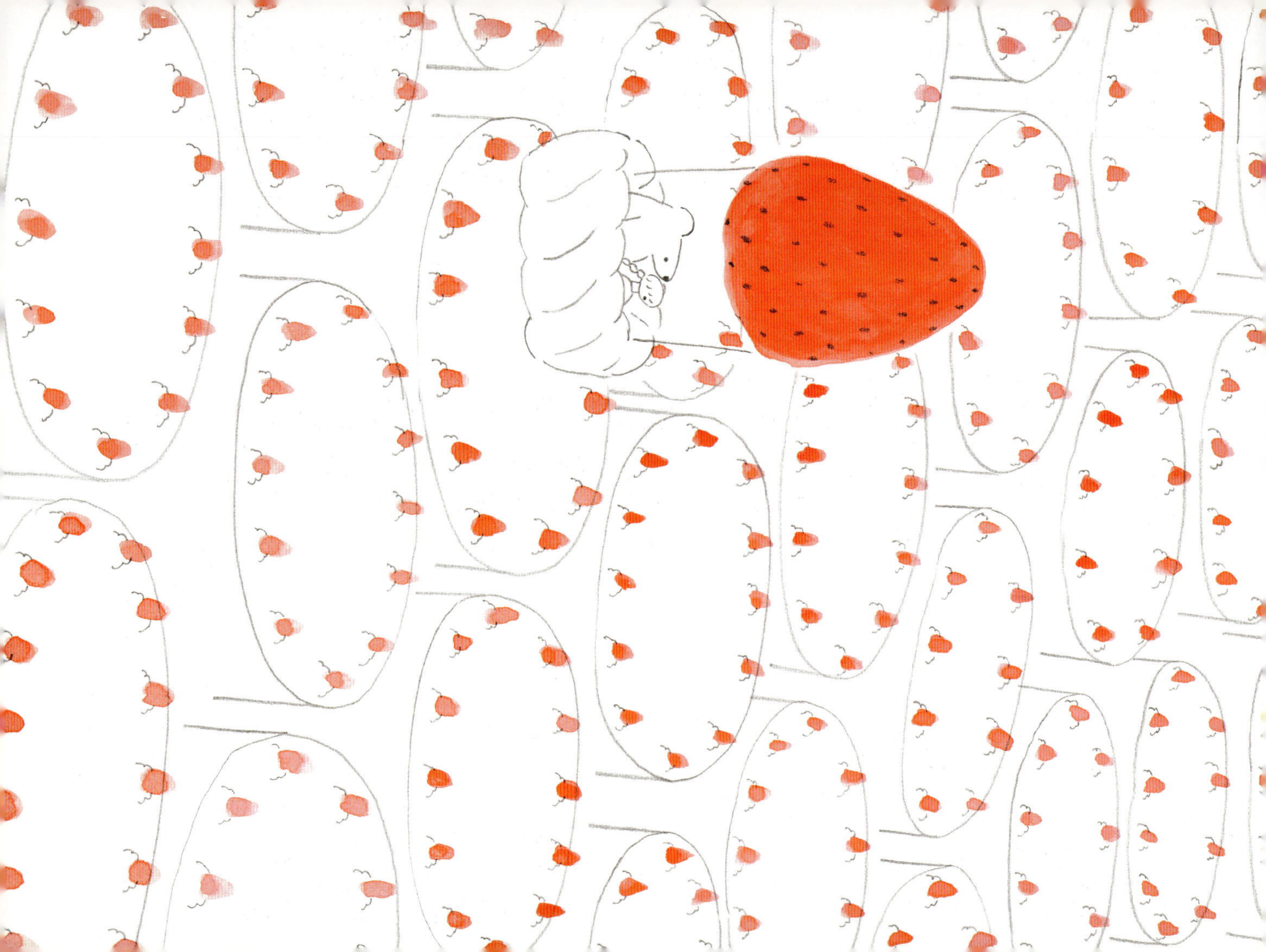

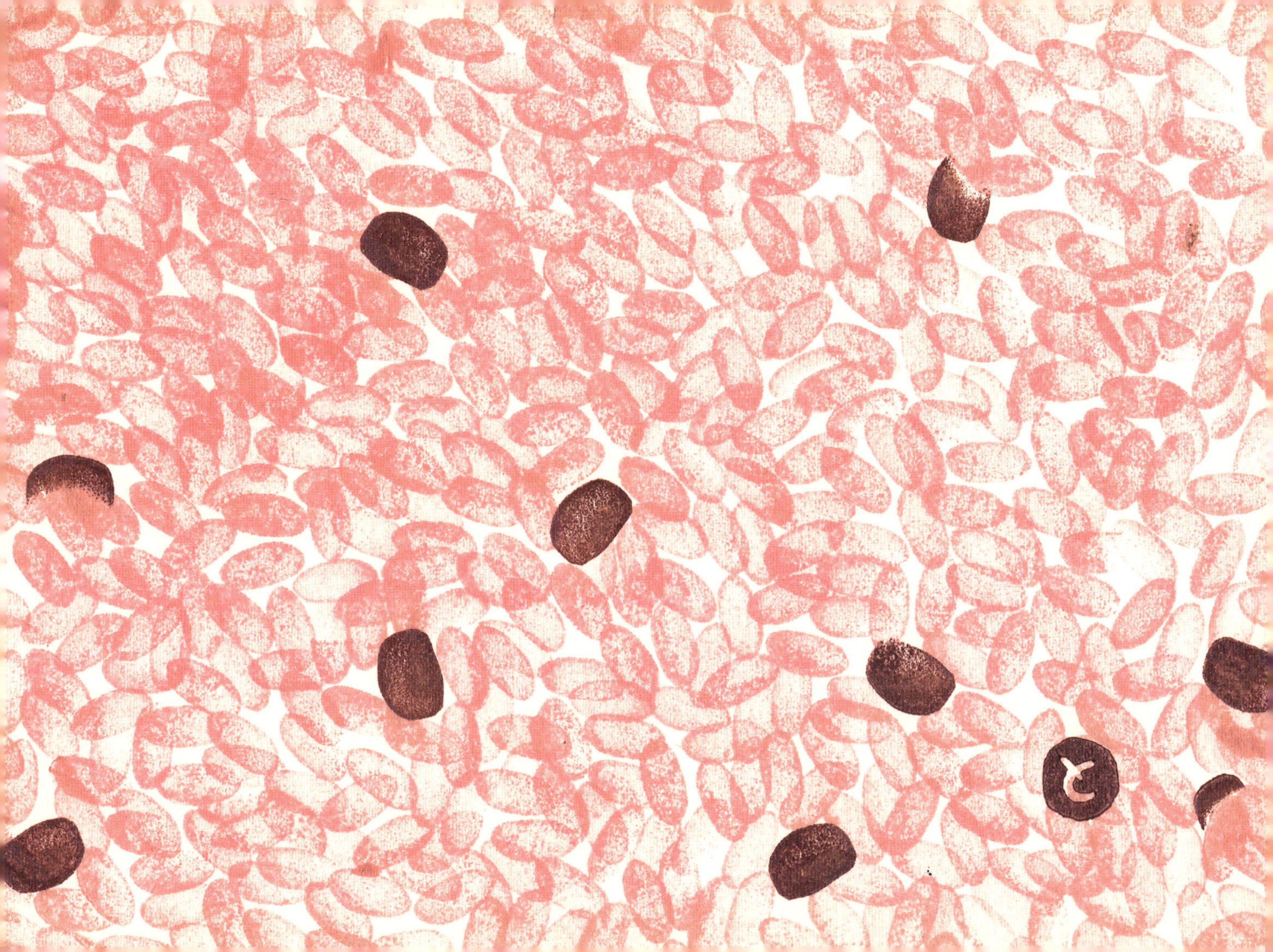

Wonder Restaurant

Chocolate Fountain

Wonder Restaurant

Tea time Cup Coffee

CURRY

CURRY

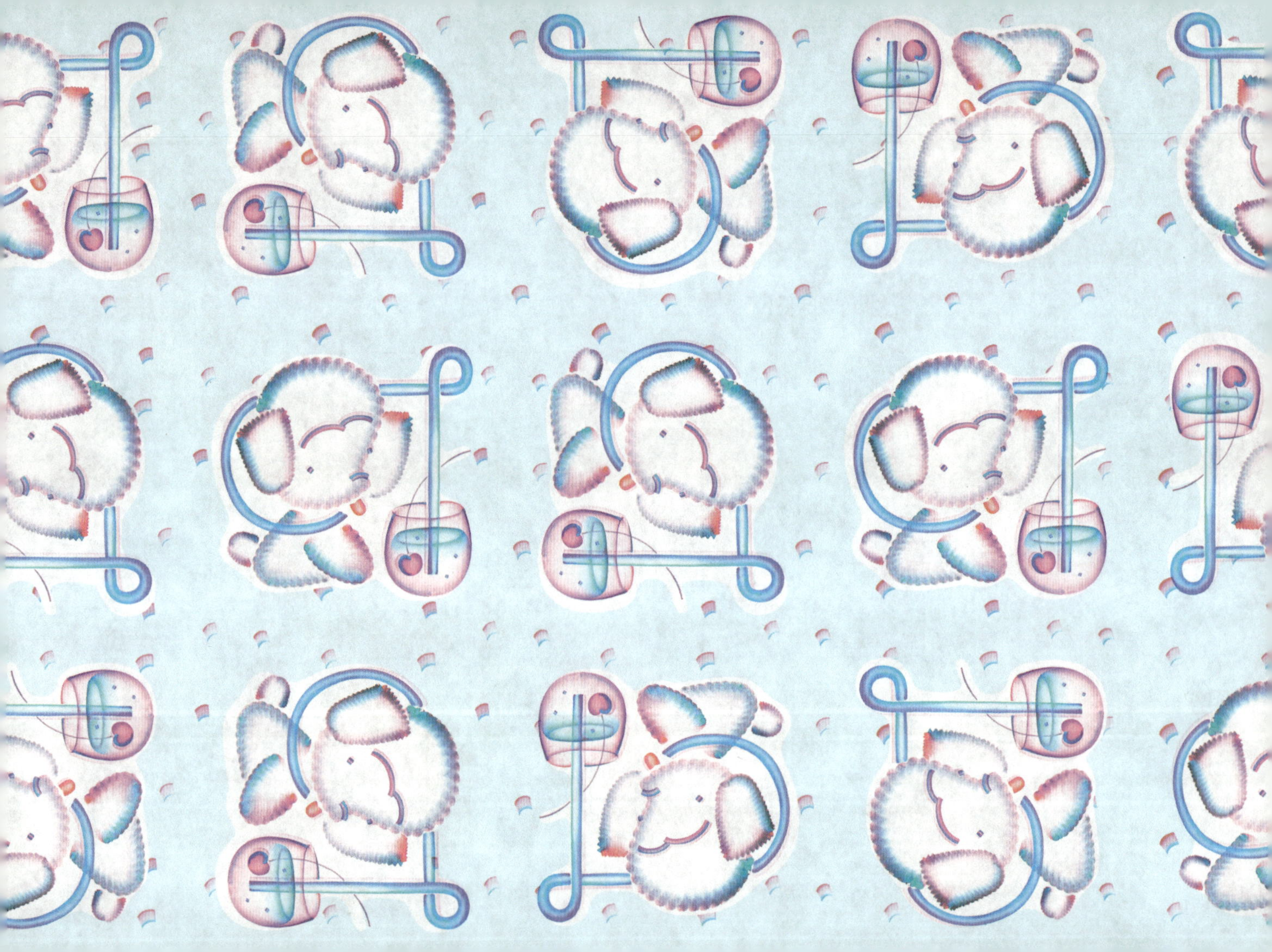

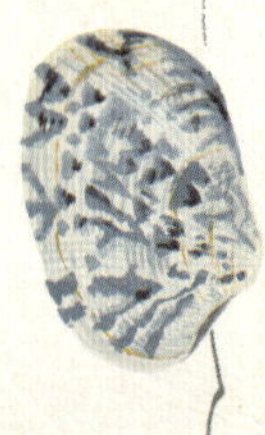

Wonder Restaurant

A Loaf of Tunnel Bread with Waiting Line